Pells

to get AHEAD

spells

to get AHEAD

Deborah Gray

FRIEDMAN/FAIRFAX

A Friedman/Fairfax Book
Friedman/Fairfax Publishers

Please visit our website:
www.metrobooks.com

This edition published by the
Michael Friedman Publishing Group,
Inc. by arrangement with The Ivy
Press Limited

2002 Friedman/Fairfax Publishers

ISBN 158663710x

A CIP record for this book
is available from the Library
of Congress

Distributed by Sterling Publishing
Company, Inc.
387 Park Avenue South
New York, NY 10016

Distributed in Canada by
Sterling Publishing
Canadian Manda Group
One Atlantic Avenue, Suite 105
Toronto, Ontario, Canada M6K 3E7

This book was conceived,
designed, and produced by
THE IVY PRESS
The Old Candlemakers
West Street
Lewes
East Sussex BN7 2NZ

Creative Director PETER BRIDGEWATER
Publisher SOPHIE COLLINS
Editorial Director STEVE LUCK
Design Manager TONY SEDDON
Senior Designer CLARE BARBER
Senior Project Editor REBECCA SARACENO
Designer JANE LANAWAY
Illustrator KIM GLASS

Printed in China
Packaging by Winner Print & Packaging

Contents

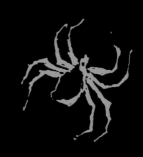

get witchy

Awaken the magical YOU

Ancient Ways
for Modern Times

The art of weaving enchantments and casting spells has
been around since at least the beginning of recorded
history—and after thousands of years of constant
refining and mastery, the magical arts are just as
powerfully effective and relevant for us
today, in our busy modern lives, as they
were back in the times of old.

★ Regardless of whether we choose to live and
work among the stress of a big bustling city,
or we prefer the quiet, laid-back style of the
countryside, our lives can be packed full of
enchanted and special moments.

★ I believe that everyone has the ability
to be a magical and empowered being, capable of
achieving their individual desires and dreams—
whether they want to attract the perfect soulmate,

Warts and
broomsticks
are *so* last
year...

rise to the top of a chosen

career, or simply learn to

connect with their inner magic

for daily relaxation, health, and harmony. The
eternal and life-affirming power of magic is
right there within us all and is just waiting
to be discovered and explored.

★ I've been casting spells since the age
of four. Some of my very first childhood
memories are of chasing fairies in my
grandmother's garden or instinctively
collecting tiny bundles of flowers and herbs
as magical offerings to the nature sprites
I could see around me everyday. Later, as an
adult, I trained with an experienced teacher of
the Old Craft, who taught in the style of an
old Druidic apprenticeship. This style puts more
emphasis on developing a "magical memory" than
on complicated rituals and overt ceremonies. My
training focused on the inner spiritual daily
practice, the power of the mind, as well as
looking at magic as a lifetime study. Over the
years, I have also studied different styles of
the craft and find it valuable to be open to
learning and incorporating both the old and
new ways into my original training.

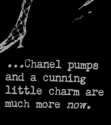

...Chanel pumps
and a cunning
little charm are
much more *now*.

ALL MODERN WITCHCRAFT IS ECLECTIC...

...and made of many different styles, so there is no one style that a witch can claim is completely pure and unchanged. Most of the ancient practices have been passed down by word of mouth and through inter-pretations of old books and family histories. As a result, there have been many modern additions to the craft.

Within this book, you'll find elements of three different kinds of craft. These are Druidism (dating back to the ancient Celts), Old European Wicca (which is based on a reverence for nature), and also traditional Folk Healing.

Magic comes easiest if you don't force it—let it flow naturally.

★ Not everyone has the time or the inclination to go to a college for witches, neither does every magical searcher want to join the local village coven—which is perfectly fine. That is why this little spell pack is indispensible. It will help to show that there's a little bit of witchiness to be found in everyone!

Everyday Magic

★ Magic happens on so many levels and in all kinds of truly amazing ways. When you learn how to unlock the eternal power of magic, fantastic and positive changes start to happen in your life. Even in our modern and sometimes very competitive and stressful lives, we can begin to get ahead of the game by casting powerful and ancient spells for success, love, and happiness. The art of magic goes back centuries and centuries, and it is not just a fairy tale or storybook fantasy. Enchantment and spellcasting can be put to very practical and effective uses in your everyday life, home, career, and personal relationships.

Even with all the wonderful magic you can muster, sometimes ... a frog is just a frog.

How to Use this Pack

This sassy spell pack is full of powerful yet simple spells and rituals, as well as sacred tools of white witchery to help you achieve your wishes and dreams and magically get ahead in every aspect of your life. Whatever your desires, there will be a spell for you to cast.

★ As you read through this book, you will learn ancient secrets of enchantment and find out the best and easiest ways of tapping into the eternal power of the magical universe.

If the vibe is right, you won't even need a wand. Unless you want one, that is.

★ I've scattered throughout this book a number of fun and effective spells that will teach you different ways of using these charming tools.

CAST THAT SPELL!

For optimum results, cast the spell at a "best time".

Included inside your spell pack are some beautiful magical tools that I've chosen especially to support and empower your journey into the world of White Magic.

MAGICAL TOOLS

In this pack you'll find three enchanted silk bags.

THE WHITE POUCH will help you enchant and store any charms for better harmony, relationships, family, and peace.

THE RED POUCH can empower and package up spell ingredients for true love, passion, vitality, and success.

THE PURPLE POUCH is perfect for stowing away the various charms and items of mystic power, psychic ability, protection, and prosperity.

★ You'll also discover a quartz crystal that's been empowered with white light to help boost any kind of spells and to surround you with lucky vibrations.

★ And lastly, let's not forget the magic potion phials which can help shake up and store many of your spellbinding recipes.

FOR EACH SPELL YOU WILL NEED...

★ ...to get a set of the ingredients, and then follow the steps carefully.

★ Now, let's start to unleash your inner magic so you too can weave the charmed life you truly deserve.

GODDESS BLESSINGS FROM DEBORAH GRAY.

get sexy

Lessons of the Love GODDESS

Seeking a Soulmate

AIM STRAIGHT FOR THE HEART

No more **sitting at** home like a wallflower; **weave** your **way to** an enchanted love life and attract your perfect match **with** the help of a magic mirror.

★ Find a place where you will be undisturbed for a few moments. Put your mirror and all your other items of enchantment onto a flat surface. Then **sit comfortably and breathe deeply for a few** moments while you let go of any negative thoughts or stressful feelings. At **this stage, focus** your thoughts on your intended loved one. If you are looking for a soulmate, simply think about the type of person who'd be a **wonderful** companion for you.

MAGICAL INGREDIENTS

★ mirror

★ red or pink lipstick or crayon

★ red candle

★ white cloth or tissue

★ some mineral or spring water

To **strengthen the power of** your spell, think about their personality and project your mind into the spiritual side of any future relationship rather than just concentrating on physical appearance and other more material matters.

CAST THAT SPELL!

Cast on the day or evening of a full or waxing moon.

If you know the name of the person you desire, first say their name seven times; if you don't know their name simply say the words, "my soulmate."

★ Then, pick up the mirror and with the lipstick or crayon draw a small heart shape onto the reflective face. Once you've done that, light the red candle and look directly into the mirror, then repeat these magical words:

"I call to thee beloved one, to cherish me more than anyone, Magic Mirror reflect my heart and send it to my love like a sacred dart. I cast this spell in the name of harmony, it shall be done, O blessed be."

★ Then, blow (or snuff) out the candle. (If you wish, you may keep the candle in a safe place and re-use it again for other love spells.)

★ Next, carefully, so as not to smudge the heart, leave the mirror somewhere near your bed for seven nights. To strengthen the power of the spell, stand near the magic mirror and think about your intended love for at least one minute on each of the seven days or nights. Finally, at the end of the seven days, pick up the mirror and wipe the heart shape off the surface with a white cloth that has been soaked in a little mineral or spring water, then say:

"The spell has been cast, the magic will last, so mote it be."

★ You can then relax, going about your everyday life and letting the magical energy do its job.

Schiaparelli's *Shocking* perfume and a well-cast spell: that should release his inner prince.

Ring Ring AN END TO PHONE AGONY

Are you hanging out for that special someone to call you on the phone? Well, waste no more time! Cast this love charm and the telephone will be ringing off the hook.

MAGICAL INGREDIENTS

★ 2 clean white cloths (scraps are fine)

★ 3 drops basil essential oil (or sprig of fresh basil leaves)

★ ¼ cup almond or apricot oil (you can use olive oil as a base—although the former leave a better fragrance for this ritual)

★ 3 drops lemongrass essential oil (or a lemongrass teabag)

★ silver spoon (plated or otherwise)

★ an eyedropper (if available)

★ To begin your spell, clean and dust off your telephone or cell phone with a dry white cloth. Then take a moment to calmly think about the person: picture their face in your mind and "see" them picking up the phone and calling you.

★ After you've performed the spell, just relax, going about your day or evening without pondering over it and sitting by the phone too much. Just let it all go now, releasing your desperation and letting the Universe do its work. Know that they will call when the time is right. Don't forget to leave your message service on when you go out and yes you may repeat the spell again, but no more than once every week otherwise you may dilute the focus and energy of the magic.

CAST THAT SPELL!

At eight in the morning or evening on any day of the week.

PERFORMING THE SPELL

★ Trickle the three drops of basil oil into the cup of base oil (or tear up the basil sprig with your hands) and say:
"By planet Mercury, I bid you to call."

★ Then trickle in the three drops of lemongrass oil, (you may instead cut open the lemongrass teabag and pour in the loose tea) into the cup of base oil, and say:
"By the wings of the messenger Mercury, I bequest you to call."

★ Stir everything together clockwise three times with a silver spoon while you say:
"By the power of messenger Mercury, you will call, so I decree, so mote it be."

★ Next, with either the eyedropper or the tip of the spoon, drizzle just one or two drops of the mixture onto a clean white cloth and wipe the cloth over the entire phone. The remainder of the mixture you can keep in the refrigerator, packaged in a clean jar, or in your potion phial with cork, to use again. The cloths you may wash or throw away.

Believe me, soon you'll be begging for it to stop.

Cherish Me More

MAN-DEVELOPMENT AT ITS FINEST

MAGICAL INGREDIENTS

★ a bunch each of...

marigolds, jasmine, lavender

★ plus some fresh leaves of...

thyme, sage, marjoram, and bay

★ terra-cotta pot (or dry hand basin)

★ generous cup salt

★ 2 dessert-spoons cinnamon powder

★ 1 dessert spoon whole cloves

To bring your partner closer and help them be more attentive, cast this spell on any clear morning of the week. Either buy the flowers needed from a shop or pick them from your garden. You'll need to lay them out to dry in the sun until the evening.

★ Put all the flowers into a terra-cotta pot or a completely dry hand basin—try to make the flowers lie in as even layers as possible. Then sprinkle the salt, cinnamon, and cloves on top.

★ Toss everything together with your hands while you say these magic words: "Turn turn, Goddess of love, mix and toss, draw down from above, future, present, and past, cherish it will be, and love will last."

★ Wash your hands well, then put a lid on the pot or place a couple of heavy books on top of the mixture in the basin and keep it there for at least a week before taking it out. This magic mixture can be kept for up to one month around your home and bedroom. Put it into earthenware or terra-cotta pots, or place in wooden bowls for a magical potpourri arrangement. You can also sprinkle the mixture underneath your bed before you and your partner make love to help boost its cherishing energy.

Tea, toast, and undying devotion. Just what I had in mind.

CAST THAT SPELL!

On the day or evening of a full or waxing moon.

Marriage Invite

If you've been dreaming for
way too long of walking down
the aisle with your true
love, but they seem to be
developing feet of clay,
then weave this charm.
So, instead of questions
like "Why are we always looking at
these stupid rings honey?", you'll
hear "Darling, how would three weeks
honeymooning in Bermuda suit you?"

Tall, dark,
handsome—and
almost ready to
shop for that
ring... Gently
does it.

★ When you are ready to start, find a
quiet place where you can be alone and put
all your spell items on a flat surface or
table. Think loving thoughts about your
partner and then take the red pen and write
both your full names next to each other on
the engagement or wedding invitations. Then
write both your names again underneath, but
this time with the first names remaining the
same but with the surnames swapped around
(your last name becomes theirs, and visa versa).

CAST THAT SPELL!

Perform the
magic ritual
itself at any
hour on a
Friday.

★ Next, place both strands of hair inside the card. Close it up and tie the card shut with the pink ribbon, then place it into the red spell pouch. Your final spell action is to put the bag in either a box or a private drawer or shelf, where it will not be disturbed or found by anyone else. Leave it to work its enchantment for however long it takes. Once the charm has worked its purpose, you can take the card out. Sprinkle it with salt to seal the spell's energy and then dispose of it any way you like. Keep the white spell bag for lots of other spells and charms.

TRUE LOVE?

Incidentally, this spell can't force anyone to marry you. No such silly sorcery! Instead, it's been magically crafted to help clear up any energy blockages or love imbalance, and the magic will only work if you two are truly meant to be life partners. So just relax and go for it. If it's true love, it will happen. If not, then you'll know when it's time to move on.

MAGICAL INGREDIENTS

★ purchase either a small engagement or a wedding invitation card (small enough to fold and fit neatly in the spell bag)

★ red pen

★ hair from your head, a hair from your lover's head (easily lifted from their comb, hair brush, or pillow)

★ piece of pink ribbon

★ the red spell bag from this spell pack

★ sprinkle of salt

Crystal Love Roses

TO BE TAKEN IN PAIRS

A powerful temptation booster! With a well-manicured hand, feed a potential or existing lover with this sweet, floral treat. This spell needs a bit of preparation, but is well worth the time.

MAGICAL INGREDIENTS

★ a few dozen red, white, or pink roses

★ couple of dishes

★ sheets of absorbent paper

★ sprinkle of superfine sugar

★ generous cup granulated sugar (table sugar)

★ ½ pint boiling water

★ pan and wooden spoon

★ shallow dishes

★ Buy a couple of dozen red, white, or pink roses (or if you are lucky enough to have a rose garden, cut them on a dry day). At midday, start the love magic by plucking off all the petals and discard the stems. Spread the petals evenly over a couple of dishes and then distribute the petals carefully over sheets of absorbent paper. Sprinkle the caster sugar over everything.

★ Next, pour the table sugar into a half pint of water and make sure the sugar melts by bringing slowly to the boil. Simmer and stir constantly with your wooden spoon until you have a firm,

CAST THAT SPELL!

Best time to cast the spell is at midday.

taffy-like mixture. You can tell when
it's ready by simply taking out the
wooden spoon and making sure there
is a little of the mixture on the
spoon. Then dip it into a bowl
of cold water. After about 30
seconds, lift out the spoon and
touch the taffy end with your
fingers; if it feels
stringy, then it's ready.

★ After the boiled
mixture is prepared, put the
rose petals into one or two
shallow dishes. Drizzle the syrup over them and
leave to soak all day and night. The next day,
spread the mixture and roses over some wire trays
and place in a cold oven, with the oven door left
open, until completely dry.

If you want him
to act right,
you need to
make sure you
feed him the
right stuff.

★ Serve the crystal roses on pretty plates or
in a wicker basket as a late-night sweetener.
These floral wonders are especially effective if
eaten while lounging sexily on a sofa, couch or—
better still, in bed.

Wee Bottle of Love

AN INSTANT CURE FOR ATTENTION DEFICIT

This is an old Scottish folk charm for the love lorn. This little bottle of love is said to awaken desire and fantasy in any man or woman who comes into contact with the wearer. Remember, each time you use this particular love potion, the magical effects last only for 24 hours, and then the rest is up to you!

Revving up for a cool night out. You've got the car, the cat, now all you need is the perfect companion.

CAST THAT SPELL!

Anytime you want to kick up your heels and get a bit of sexy attention.

MAGICAL INGREDIENTS

★ 7 drops musk essence or oil

★ 7 drops vanilla essence or oil

★ 7 drops sandalwood essence or oil

★ 3 drops bergamot essence or oil

★ 3 drops mandarin (or orange) essence or oil

★ 3 drops rose geranium essence or oil

★ ½ cup almond or apricot oil

★ bowl

★ glass jar or perfume bottle

★ red or purple cloth

★ pink paper

★ Mix everything together in a bowl and then pour the mixture into a clean glass jar or perfume bottle. Put a red or purple cloth over the top and leave it to settle for three days.

★ Then, on any night or day you wish to go out for a hot date, dab a little on your wrists and sprinkle a few drops over a piece of pink paper where you have written the words:

"Let the games begin, having fun is not a sin."

You may want to accessorize your spell with a little retail therapy. Take a friend to carry your bags.

★ Wrap the paper up in a ball and leave under your bed for at least one day and night.

Passion Potion

MIX UP SOME
MUTUAL ATTRACTION

To send sexual temperatures soaring and boost your romance factor, cast this spell just before your lover is expected home. Don't forget to have a luxurious bath or shower (preferably with your partner) using your sexiest bath lotions and perfumes and get dressed up in your most bewitching and skimpy lingerie.

MAGICAL INGREDIENTS

★ 1 bottle vanilla essence

★ 1 bottle musk essential oil

★ 1 bottle geranium essential oil

★ 1 glass orange juice

★ 1 balloon

★ cotton buds

★ red or white ribbon

★ rose petals

★ Place all your spell ingredients onto a table (or the floor), with the inflated balloon in the center and the bottles arranged evenly around it— vanilla and musk on the left, geranium and orange juice on the right. Dip the cotton bud stick into the geranium essence to gather up some of the oil and then wipe it around the balloon once. Then dip the bud into the vanilla essence and wipe it around the balloon. Next dip the cotton bud into the musk oil and wipe that around the balloon as well. Finally, dip the bud into the juice and wipe the last circle around the balloon to bind the magical energies.

★ Next, tie the balloon with a red or white ribbon onto the end of your bed and leave it there for the whole evening.

★ Sprinkle some rose petals over your sheets and get yourself ready for a hot evening of passion with your partner.

CAST THAT SPELL!

The best time to cast the spell is early evening.

Look in the mirror... and see someone irresistible gazing into your eyes!

29

Romance Return

REKINDLE
OLD FLAMES

If you wish to be back in the arms of an ex-lover, cast this spell at seven o'clock on any morning of the year.

MAGICAL INGREDIENTS

★ pinch of marjoram
★ pinch of salt
★ cup of red wine
★ red cloth
★ 3 violets
★ about 8 inches of copper wire

★ In the morning, place all your spell ingredients on a flat surface near a window or a doorway and sit nearby, breathing calmly and deeply for a few moments to settle your energies. Think about your ex-lover, picturing their face in your mind, and send them loving and peaceful thoughts. Sprinkle the marjoram and next the salt into the red wine, then cover the cup with the red cloth and leave it where it is for the whole day.

CAST THAT SPELL!

Best time to cast the spell is at seven o'clock in the morning.

★ That evening at seven o'clock, take off the cloth from the cup and dip your index finger into the red wine mixture, then, with the same finger, draw the initials of your ex-lover onto the cloth. Next, place all the violets onto the cloth and roll everything up into a small bundle. After that, wrap the copper wire around the cloth and either leave the bundle near a window or leave it outside all evening to be charged by the energy of the moon.

★ The next morning (any time before midday), unwrap the cloth. Dispose of both the copper wire and the red cloth into the trash can but keep hold of the violets. Sprinkle the flowers on a stretch of earth or a garden near your house.

A fit of vapors won't get you your mate. Dry your eyes, then mix up a spell and win him right back.

Mini Charms and Quick Tips

MOON WEAVING

Each lunar cycle and phase brings opportunities to weave certain spells—and the most popular by far are charms for romantic endeavors.

NEW MOON ★ gives wonderful lunar energies to help kick-start new relationships or to bring brand-new passions and excitement into well-worn partnerships.

WAXING (OR GROWING) MOON ★ gives space for strengthening and developing affairs of the heart and boosts commitment and marriage vows.

FULL MOON ★ the numero uno witchy time for any kind of love spell—but especially to hoist up to the next level of intimacy and to weave charms to attract soulmates.

WANING (OR SHRINKING) MOON ★ gives the perfect opportunity to get rid of bad old love habits (like banishing jealousy and nagging) and to well and truly get over an old flame.

DARK MOON ★ not an easy time for love spells, but this is an excellent phase to let you take time out for yourself, and reflect on what you would like in your love life for the future. This will prepare you for a new beginning in the coming new moon phase.

CHARM COLLECTION

If you always want to remain a love diva
and you have the knack of collecting, then
you better start collecting some of these.

★ Gather together
some new and antique
perfume bottles—a must
if you want to start
mixing up your own
magic scents and love
potions.

★ Make sure you
have some mirrors
of various shapes
and sizes around
your bedroom and
bathroom. They are
constantly being
used in rituals for
romance.

★ Set up a love
altar for yourself in
your bedroom. Design
it yourself so it can
be very light and
"goddess friendly"
rather than dark and
Buffyesque (don't want
to scare off that shy
new beau now do we?).
Dress it up with
gloriously scented
potpourri (my favorite
is a combination of
dried jasmine, orange
peel, and rose), and
add a pretty goddess
statue if you like.

★ Sprinkle
around a few rose
quartz crystals
and, of course,
your tumble stone
crystal and the red
(color of love)
spell bag from
this spell pack.

★ Gather some
gorgeously scented
love candles in
red, pink, or
pastel shades or
pale violet, peach,
and lavender.

★ Fill up a vase
with fresh water and
keep it filled with
at least one or two
fresh flowers every
few days.

get lucky

Find your pot of GOLD

Business Charmer

HARD-WORKING
SORCERY

Cast this spell when you'd like your business to attract more customers, clients, or contacts. It can also replenish the level of good luck in your home, office, or working environment.

CAST THAT SPELL!

Cast your spell on any Sunday, preferably in the sunlight.

MAGICAL INGREDIENTS

★ business, bank, or property items

★ piece of green material or scarf

★ 1 cinnamon stick

★ 3 cloves

★ mortar and pestle (or electric grinder)

★ 1 peppermint incense stick (or peppermint essence and oil burner)

★ For ultimate effect, you should bless your bankcards and business documents with this magical mixture. So gather together any or all of your business cards (you can also add any of your business proposals or contracts, or even lease and property documents), then wrap one or more of them up in a green scarf. Place the cinnamon stick and cloves into the mortar and grind with the pestle (or use your electric grinder) until you have a powdery mixture.

★ Place the bundle onto a flat surface and sprinkle the magic mixture over the top. Then, light the stick of peppermint incense (or oil burner) and breathe calmly and deeply as you visualize meeting new people, sitting in business meetings, having successful talks and customers or clients calling for appointments. Keep your thoughts in a positive and upbeat state as you repeat this incantation:

The one-minute (magical) manager knows that a neat spell is worth a dozen business manuals.

"Fortunata, Goddess of luck and prosperity, bring good fortune now to me, business is boosted, my clients are lining up by three times three. Blessings returned to the universe, so will it be."

★ Leave everything as it is until the incense or oil mixture has burned completely down. Then unwrap the bundlle, wipe up the residue mixture, and clean everything up. Put your cards and documents back where you normally store them.

Car Tonic

THE *TRULY EFFECTIVE*
VANISHING CREAM

When it's time to trade in that aging
auto for a snazzy new number, don't just
salivate over the pages of the sports
car manual—cast this spell and sell that
old motor in a flash.

MAGICAL INGREDIENTS

★ the crystal
from your
spell pack

★ glass of
spring or
mineral water

★ a moon guide
or almanac
(fishing guides
can also be
handy for
checking moon
times)

Wave goodbye to
the rustbucket;
say hello to
the Porsche.

★ What you need to do is brew up some moon
water to wash and purify your car's aura. The
mystical force of the moon can help bring balance
and cosmic alignment into a magic ritual, and is
especially effective when you combine
it with water and quartz crystal.

★ So, on the night you intend to cast the spell, put your spell pack crystal into a glass and fill it up with either the spring or mineral water. At exactly the stroke of midnight, place the glass outside or near a window so that the moon's rays can charge the crystal and water and leave it there all night. Make sure no-one will kick it over, or hurt themselves. Don't worry if it unexpectedly rains that night, it won't ruin anything.

★ The next morning when you wake up, gather up the glass and hold it in both hands, saying:
"Goddess Luna, I thank you for aid."

★ Both the crystal and the water are now filled with maximum lunar potency. Take out the crystal and keep it in a safe place (the moon-charged crystal can help you with lots of other kinds of spells too!). When you wash the car that day, mix all of the moon water into the last bucket of rinse water and slosh it over the car, then dry it off with a new or completely clean cloth.

CAST THAT SPELL!

Best time to cast the spell is at midnight, on a clear night. Even better if it's a night with a full moon, in which case, find out the exact time the moon turns full and then begin the spell.

Lucky Streak

BAD LUCK IS FOR ORDINARY PEOPLE

This fabulous lucky spell helps to quell feelings of insecurity and bad fortune and replace them with abundance and confidence...

CAST THAT SPELL!

The best time to cast the spell is during a new moon.

★ Place the candle that represents you in the center of a table or a flat surface and then put the purple candle on the left-hand side, the white candle on the right-hand side, and finally the gold candle in front of the center candle. Then sprinkle the coriander around you in a clockwise circle.

MAGICAL INGREDIENTS

★ 1 candle in your favorite color to represent yourself

★ 1 purple candle

★ 1 white candle

★ 1 gold candle

★ 1 teaspoon coriander seeds (or fresh cilantro leaves)

★ enough candlesticks for each candle

PERFORMING THE SPELL

To begin, light the candle that represents you and say these words aloud:
"Candle of the center Goddess, you are me, your form is my form, your name is [say your own name]."

Then light the purple candle and say the following words aloud:
"Candle of the left Goddess, you are my fears and insecurity, now you are leaving me, I wish you farewell."

Next, ignite the gold candle and say:
"Candle of the golden Goddess, you are my energy and courage, now you grow and strengthen, I bring you close to my heart."

Light the white candle and say:
"Candle of the right Goddess, you are renewal and opportunities, you are welcome here on this sacred night."

Now sit still for a few moments. Close your eyes and chant these words at least seven times:
"Planet Mercury, open the way, O blessed be."

When you've finished, blow or snuff out the candles and sweep up the coriander seeds or cilantro leaves. The energy you've raised from this ritual will flow into the universe, so now you can relax and let the magic go free. Cast this spell again whenever you feel like a boost of good luck, but not more than once a month (otherwise you can diffuse the magical energy).

Dice Days

Before you buy a lottery ticket or enter a raffle, cast this lucky charm and better your chances at winning in the games. When taking risks with money, don't forget the "good witch's rule," which is to only play with spare change or money you can afford to lose.

MAGICAL INGREDIENTS

★ 3 coins of the same denomination

★ box (can be wooden or cardboard)

★ set of dice

★ 3 aces from a pack of playing cards

★ green ribbon

★ and some mint tea

★ First, gather together all your items of enchantment and place them onto a table or flat surface. Then, throw the three coins until you get either all three heads or three tails. You may want to throw them onto a cushion to stop them from rolling away too far. Leave the coins near the box and then throw the two dice until you're able to get both dice adding up to the number seven.

CAST THAT SPELL!

Begin your lucky spell at nine in the morning, or nine in the evening on any day of the week.

✭ Next, pick up the three aces and hold them in both hands as you let go of negative thoughts and repeat this magic chant: "Lucky nine and lucky seven grant me wealth that's sent from heaven, O mote it be."

✭ Place all the coins, dice, and cards into the box, then wrap the green ribbon around it and place the box somewhere near your money documents for at least seven days.

EXTRA LUCK

To bring extra luck to your enchantment, first make some mint tea and let it cool to room temperature. Dip both your hands into the tea and then wipe them dry with a clean white cloth.

You may want to entrust your winnings to your favorite, extra-special banker...

Back on Track

GETTING
AHEAD IN THE
WORKPLACE

Are you stumped as to what kind of career you should go into? Or perhaps you would like to dust off your attitude about work in general and get some fresh ideas and motivation? If that sounds like you, then cast this spell.

Keep your witchy qualities hidden from your work colleagues. It's better that they think you are diabolically clever without outside assistance.

★ Just before bed, take a shower or bath using the herbal soap or shower gel to cleanse your body and aura. While showering, imagine you're washing away all past worries or stress down the drain. After patting yourself dry, put on a clean robe or if the night is warm enough, remain skyclad (witches' term for "naked") and gather the spell items near the bathroom sink.

CAST THAT SPELL!
On any Sunday evening.

★ Light the stick of sandalwood incense and breathe in the aroma for a moment. Take the cork stopper out of the potion phial and pop in both the lemon and orange seeds. Then, using either an eyedropper or the end of a teaspoon, drizzle in a couple of drops of vanilla essence. Next, put the cork stopper back and look in the bathroom mirror as you shake the phial gently and say:

"I shake the charm to have a notion,
I shake the charm to make a potion,
where can my direction be?
Spinner of dreams now help me see."

★ For the final part of the spell, place the magic potion on a table or in a drawer near your bed and leave it there for 21 days. In that time, take note of any strong dreams, ideas, or visions you might have that could give you some signals. Whenever you are meditating in your room, have the phial somewhere nearby to aid you in getting your career back on track.

ON THE 22ND DAY

On the 22nd day you can empty the potion phial. Wash it out with warm soapy water. Leave it open for a day to dry completely so you can use it for other kinds of spells and charms.

MAGICAL INGREDIENTS

★ some herbal soap or some shower gel

★ 1 stick of sandalwood incense

★ empty potion phial from your spell pack

★ 1 bottle of vanilla essence

★ 1 orange seed

★ 1 lemon seed

Win Win

BEND THE RULES
BEFORE THE GAME

If you want to have the winning edge in any kind of competitions— be they sport, or school- or work-based—then cast this easy charm and get ready to enter the winner's circle.

There's nothing like a little unfair advantage.

MAGICAL INGREDIENTS

★ 1 glass of ginger beer or ginger-flavored tea

★ blue or white candle

★ ground nutmeg

CAST THAT SPELL!

Just before the competition.

★ At a convenient time before your competition begins, get dressed in what you are going to be wearing and put your spell items on a flat surface or table. Put the candle in a candle-stick and light it. Then sprinkle the nutmeg powder around yourself in a counterclockwise circle and say:

"I now send away any doubts or fears, only the warrior remains."

★ Then sprinkle the nutmeg in a clockwise
circle around you and say:

"I am the warrior, there's nothing I cannot do,
I am the tiger, watch me roar!"
(then let out a great big tiger's roar)

Be sure to
be generous in
your success.
Gloat with
your friends.

★ Finally, take a sip of the
ginger tea or beer. Blow out the
candle, and say, "It is so."

GO FOR GOLD
You can get changed
into your normal
clothes if you
like, or just leave
the same gear on,
and get ready to
go for gold!

Job Hunt
IT'S ALL TO DO
WITH ATTITUDE

Get ready for
a meteoric rise.
Headhunters will
be ringing your
number when you
work this
influential
spell.

Do you picture yourself breaking through
the glass ceiling of a giant corporation,
being the head of your project team,
or simply being able to find a job that
suits *your* hours and *your*
lifestyle? Get yourself
into a positive mind
state for job-hunting
and clever career moves
by collecting the
magical ingredients
for this spell.

CAST THAT SPELL!
The best time
to cast the
spell is in
the evening
of either a new
or full moon.

★ To begin your enchanted job search, place your spell items onto a flat surface or table. After you've lit the candle, stir together the parsley and rosemary into a small bowl and let yourself feel

uplifted, positive, and focused on getting the career and job you desire. Really visualize the picture of proudly sitting in your new to-die-for office, getting along famously with influential people, climbing that ladder to success, and gaining recognition for all your hard work. And then say these words:

"Spirit of prosperity, surround me with good luck
O blessed be.
I am where I want to be,
I feel it and trust it and nothing can stop me,
so mote it be."

MAGICAL INGREDIENTS

★ 1 candle
★ 1 sprig or teaspoon of parsley (dried or fresh)
★ 1 sprig or teaspoon of rosemary
★ small bowl
★ crystal from your spell pack
★ blue material or paper
★ white bag from your spell pack

Creative Crystal FOR THE ARTIST WITHIN

MAGICAL INGREDIENTS

★ a comfortable place to sit

★ the crystal from your spell pack

You'll get the strangest urge to work a magical transformation on even the most ordinary, *everyday* things.

If you fancy trying something new—a different hobby or art and craft—but can't seem to take the final step, then maybe you could do with a little help to get you going. Cast this spell to stimulate your creative and artistic abilities.

CAST THAT SPELL!
On a Sunday or a Monday evening.

PERFORMING THE SPELL

Find a tranquil place where you can meditate undisturbed for at least a half-hour. Sit on a chair or on some comfy cushions on the floor. Let the crystal sit neatly in both hands and relax your body and mind while you breathe deeply and evenly for a few moments.

Next, let your mind become still and free of negative thoughts and stress. Close your eyes, and imagine that you are floating through the air, your body feeling lighter and lighter and more and more relaxed and at peace. If you start to feel nervous about floating away, just lightly squeeze the crystal in your hands; this will help ground you to the room and keep you feeling safe.

When you're ready, start to think about the type of art you've always wanted to do. If it's music, let yourself hear music (hum or sing if you like). If it's painting, float through hundreds of

Write that poem, paint that picture; this spell brings out your inner genius.

shades of colors and pictures. Whatever you desire, let yourself go there, imagine and experience it. When you feel inspired and ready to come back, just squeeze the crystal three times and open your eyes. Keep sitting down for a moment until you get your bearings and then go about your day, uplifted and energized. Whenever you want a surge of creativity, repeat this beautiful ritual as many times as you like.

Mini Charms and Quick Tips

LUCKY TIPS

★ When casting spells for better fortune and success, it really helps if you understand the basic tools of the magical trade, such as the different effects of lucky numbers, colors, and candle powers. Once you know about these things, you are open to a whole new area for playing in!

★ DON'T GET CAUGHT going skyclad (witches' term for "naked") at work...they won't understand!

★ A LIST OF LUCKY ITEMS... a four-leaf clover, candles, stars (very lucky), moons (full and new), mint leaves, nutmeg, rosemary, the number seven, horseshoes.

MAGICAL NUMBERS

Magical numbers can tell you a wealth about people's characters, traits, and interests...

1 independence, self-assurance, ego, lucidity

2 ability to share, togetherness, reconciliation

3 triple goddess, increase development, good fortune

4 strong foundations, sound, stable, efficient, hard work

5 communicating, acceleration, expression, discussion, travel

6 family, love and happiness, indulgence, household

7 mysticism, psychic ability, guardian angels, spirit force, precognitive, clairvoyance

8 extremes, vigor, concentration, victory, or defeat

9 forgiveness, tenderness, group therapy, social work, luck

10 fulfillment, oneness, conclusion, judgement

ASTRO CANDLES

★ In the ancient art of magic, each of the 12 star signs of the zodiac are aligned with certain colors, talismans, crystals, and candles. Here is a very handy list of candle colors that can help you strengthen the effect of the spells or rituals you perform. Simply look up your star sign to find the perfect enchanted candle for your own altar or charm table.

ARIES white, rosy pink
TAURUS deep red, pale lemon
GEMINI vermillion, light blue
CANCER turquoise, earth brown
LEO deep green, bright red
VIRGO gold, dark and light blue
LIBRA violet, red
SCORPIO magenta, purple
SAGITTARIUS burnished gold, green
CAPRICORN white, bright pink
AQUARIUS aqua blue, silver
PISCES sea green, purple

get happy
and healthy

Bewitching BREWS

Witch's Kitchen
HUBBLE, BUBBLE:
CULINARY MAGIC

Here is an old magical recipe for "Merry Bread" to enchant and bring happy vibes to your favorite dinner guests and family.

MAGICAL INGREDIENTS

★ wooden spoon

★ big mixing bowl

★ 2 cups lukewarm whole or lowfat milk

★ 2 sachets of dry active yeast

★ 1 teaspoon salt

★ ½ cup honey

★ ¼ cup brown sugar

★ dish towel

★ Mix everything together slowly in the bowl until the ingredients are combined nicely. Then cover up the bowl with a dish towel and put it in a warm place (such as a sunny window shelf or a cozily heated room). In a half-hour or so, look to see if the mixture has doubled in size. Wait until it has and then mix in these next ingredients:

2 free range eggs, 3 tablespoons soft butter, 2 cups all-purpose white flour

★ Then stir the mixture with your wooden spoon (or a fork) and when it starts to bubble up, mix in:

4 tablespoons diced, mixed dried fruit (or plain raisins if you prefer), 3 cups wholewheat flour, 1 cup wheat germ, 2 tablespoons of poppy seeds (or sesame seeds if you prefer), 1⅓ cups rolled oats

★ Next, cover your hands (make sure they're clean and dry first) with some of the all-purpose flour, and start kneading the bread slowly and carefully, sprinkling in a

CAST THAT SPELL!

Any time you feel like cooking some of this wonderful, mouth-watering bread.

little extra all-purpose flour if you must, until the dough is no longer sticky and feels stretchy and smooth to touch. While you knead the dough, focus on happy thoughts and repeat these words out loud:

"Stir and mix, mix and stir,
enchantment and happiness,
are now incurred, merry magic,
magic merry, O blessed be the harvest."

★ Put the mixture into a greased bowl, then cover with a clean dish towel and put it back into a warm place for at least an hour. When it has doubled again in size, beat the dough down with your fist a couple of times (bonus stress therapy!). Then break into two, and mold the two pieces with your hands into rounded or oblong shapes. Place both of them onto a greased baking sheet and cover with the towel again, then leave in a warm place until they double in size once more. Then bake in a preheated oven at 350°F for 50 to 60 minutes or until ready (stick a skewer or knife into the middle and it should come out clean).

★ Bring it out of the oven with your oven mitts, then let it cool off on the sheet or scoop up onto a plate and serve hot and sliced up with a delicious spoonful of apricot jelly or a swipe of butter with a dash of brown sugar sprinkled on top.

Fire burn, cauldron bubble... Accessorize your domestic goddess with a cute bandanna and you're all ready to cook up a storm.

Solar Power

HARNESS THE SUN'S ENERGY

This beautiful and simple sun charm will help attract harmony and the healing power of loving energy to yourself and others.

★ If you can, try to repeat this spell at least once every year, on any day after the full moon. It can really give you and your loved ones a well-needed boost, and it is a very simple and uplifting ritual.

★ On the day, set your alarm at least 20 minutes before the sun rises to give yourself a chance to wake up. Drink a glass of water with fresh lemon to clear your head.

★ Begin the ritual at the exact time of sunrise. Simply go outside or stand at a window facing the sun. Stand holding one of your favorite flowers (my personal favorite is one spectacular golden sunflower, but choose any kind of flower you like).

CAST THAT SPELL!

Best time to cast the spell is any early morning, at sunrise.

MAGICAL INGREDIENT

★ your favorite flower

This spell works on everyone you love, whether they're right there at home with you or far away. It's a real heart-warmer.

PERFORMING THE SPELL

★ Hold one or two flowers in both hands and say these words aloud:

"To the God and Goddess of the Sun, your healing rays are with me now. From this day we exist as one as together we radiate our shining power.

Every morning and every day, I shall celebrate your immortal way. We shine as one, It will be so and so it is."

★ To release the glimmering energy into the universe and to strengthen the karmic power of this beautiful spell, give your flower power away later in the day to a friend, lover, or someone who is a bit down on their luck, as an unselfish and special gift.

★ As you give it to them, say just these words,

"Here is a magic flower of the sun to brighten your day."

★ If the person is a bit conservative, you don't need to go into the fine details of your spellcasting. Just a simple "I picked out this flower just for you" will suffice. And if you are a bit shy of going up and personally giving it to someone, you can deliver (or send by courier) the flower in a nice box with a little card or note attached, which has the same words, "Here is a magic flower of the sun to brighten your day."

★ The results may well amaze you in the most delightful way.

Face Facts

...WITH CLEAR SKIN AND A WINNING SMILE

To enliven both the inner and outer beauty of your face and skin, you may cast this spell any time when the sun is out in the day and during a waxing (growing) or new moon.

CAST THAT SPELL!

At any time on a sunny day and during a waxing (growing) or new moon.

MAGICAL INGREDIENTS

★ iron pot
★ spring water
★ 3 silver-colored coins
★ pinch of dried or fresh lavender
★ sprig of mint
★ your purple bag from the spell pack

★ Fill an iron pot full of water and then drop three silver-colored coins into the pot. Throw in a pinch of dried or fresh lavender and mint, then leave the pot in the sun all day and at night leave it under the light of the moon.

★ At midday on the following day, peer into the pot at your own reflection and then dip your hands in, gathering up hand-fulls of water and splashing it over your arms and your face. Allow yourself to feel more fresh and beautiful as you absorb the radiant energy of both the moon and sun.

Happiness is just
so contagious! Take
your new, confident
beauty out and enjoy
the world.

★ To lengthen and enrich
the overall power of the
spell, tip the water out
over a flower garden or near
a lovely tree.

★ The leftover coins are
to be kept in your purple
spell bag for 21 days.
Then, once the spell has
served its purpose,
you may put the coins
back in your wallet or
coin purse and spend
them at any time.

Hair Today, Long Tomorrow

RAPUNZEL-LIKE LOCKS CAN BE YOURS

MAGICAL INGREDIENTS

- ★ scissors
- ★ glass or china bowl
- ★ 1 egg
- ★ 1 tablespoon mayonnaise
- ★ 1 teaspoon olive oil (if your hair is very dry, make it a tablespoon) OR
- ★ if your hair is oily, leave out the olive oil altogether and add 1 teaspoon of lemon juice instead
- ★ 2 tablespoons unflavored full-fat yogurt

To help make your hair grow longer and faster, try this divine hair magic and you'll be looking like Lady Rapunzel in no time!

★ At either midday or midnight, light the candle and then snip off a tiny piece of your hair with scissors (a half inch of just a few strands will do) and place the hair in the bowl. Next, break the egg into the bowl (excluding the shell) and say the following words:

"O Artemis who attends both wood and glade, I bid you here while this spell is made."

CAST THAT SPELL!

Weave the charm on the day or evening of a full moon.

★ Then stir in the mayonnaise along with either the olive oil or lemon juice and say:

"Shining Goddess hear my story,
I wish to enchant this crowning glory."

★ Then mix in the yogurt and dip your hands in the mixture. Start applying the luscious ingredients over your scalp and hair right down to the ends. When all the mixture is on the hair say:

"In the name of good the spell is done,
and now the magic has begun."

★ Wrap your hair up in a towel and sit quietly, breathing calmly, with the mixture left on for 20 minutes. When the time is up, wash your hair thoroughly with shampoo (if you condition it, make sure you use a very lightweight and non-greasy one).

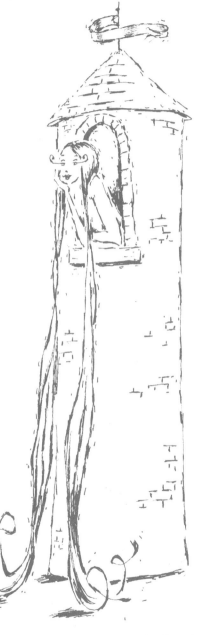

Now you've got the hair—all you need is the tower (and the prince).

Glamour Petals

HOW TO GET
THAT HOLLYWOOD
AURA

The art of bewitchery is full of glamour. And the Goddess Venus is just the diva you can call on for a dose of charisma and star power. If you feel like a beauty boost, weave this spell at dawn on Friday.

MAGICAL INGREDIENTS

★ mirror
★ 3 orchids or 3 gardenias
★ glass vase
★ white bag from the spell pack

★ Find a quiet space where you can be alone and uninterrupted. Take a relaxing bath or shower and then either remain skyclad (witches' term for "naked") or get dressed in something that makes you feel great. Place the flowers in a glass vase and the mirror close by so you can see your reflection. Sit or kneel comfortably in front of the vase and gently remove one of the flowers. Stroke the petals softly around your face. As you move it up and down and around your cheeks and lips, feel the beauty and radiant force within the flower flowing into you.

CAST THAT SPELL!

The best time to cast the spell is on a Friday at sunrise.

★ Next, close your eyes and say these magic words:

"O gracious Muse, bestow on me: beauty, charm, and grace."

★ Now open your eyes, smell the scent of the flower, breathe in its luscious aroma. Let it fill up your soul and say:

"Great Goddess, give glamour to my word, body, and face!"

★ Then hold the flower above your head, pointing to the sky, and say:

"In the presence of this most mythic dawn, great beauty and glamour will become my form."

★ Still holding the flower in your hands before you, gaze at your reflection in the mirror and say:

"The spell has been cast. So shall it be.

★ Then take out the other flowers and pluck the petals off, throwing away the stems and wrapping the petals up in pink tissue paper. Put this into your white bag from the spell pack. Carry them around with you at any time during the next month for an extra boost of confidence. The glamour petals themselves will last for only one month, but their magical effects will last for as long as you wish.

★ After one month, open the bag and throw the old petals into a stretch of water, such as the sea or a swimming pool, and thank the Goddess Venus for lending you her magical energies. This spell can be cast once every three months for another beauty boost.

Just add an appropriate escort and shimmy on out there.

Hourglass Shaper

TRULY A
MAGICAL
FAT-BURNER

Yes, you are definitely applauded for starting that fantastic new fitness campaign to whip that body of yours into shape. And here's some magical help to slim down your waist and thighs with spellbinding results.

All the witchery you need to gain (and maintain) a goddess-like form.

MAGICAL INGREDIENTS

★ long piece of naturally colored cheesecloth (enough to wrap around your waist and hips like a bandage)

★ 1 cup black iced coffee

★ bowl or pot

★ 2 small bells (these can be bronze, any type of metal, china, or glass)

CAST THAT SPELL!

Best performed during the phase of a waning moon (as the moon appears to shrink, hopefully so will your butt!).

⭐ Gather all your ingredients and lay them on a flat surface, like a vanity table or the floor in your bathroom. Dip the cheesecloth into the iced coffee and while it is soaking, take a long relaxing bath or shower. When you are done, dry yourself and remain skyclad.

⭐ Go over to your bathroom mirror and wrap the coffee-soaked cheesecloth around your waist and thighs. Then ring the bell three times while you stand for a few moments and say these words:

"As the moon wanes, so shall I,
O great Isis, your energy shall fly.
My body is strong and serves me well,
I am grateful and calm, O blessed be."

AFTER-CARE

Now that the ritual is finished you may wash the cheesecloth with soap and water and hang it out to dry to use next month if you plan to repeat the spell. Or you can simply throw it away.

⭐ Sit down cross-legged for a few moments, until the cheesecloth feels a similar temperature to that of your body. Then unravel the cloth and wipe down your body with a damp towel. Afterwards, get dressed as normal.

Good Witch's Bottle

FOR HOME
INSURANCE

Brush away those
cobwebs! This is
sparkling *clean*
domestic magic.

To help bring peaceful **vibrations** and to harmonize the energies of your home, why not make up your very own "magic lantern"?

> **CAST THAT SPELL!**
>
> At six o'clock on a Sunday evening.

★ Gather all the ingredients, and start by placing the powdered onion into the bowl and say:
"By the power of one, this onion protects my home and all who reside within."

★ Then, sprinkle a teaspoon of the rosemary in the bowl:
"By the power of two this rosemary heals my home and all who reside within."

★ Next, add the ground ginger and say:
"By the power of three this ginger will energize my home and all my family and friends within."

★ Add the dill and say:
"By the power of four this dill fortifies my home and all who reside and **visit** within."

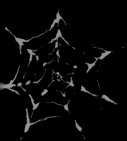

★ Add the white pepper to the mixture and say:
"By the power of five, this pepper defends my home and all who reside within."

★ Add the aniseed and say:
"By the power of six, this aniseed invigorates my home and all within."

★ And finally, the teaspoon of earth:
"By the power of seven, this earth protects my home and family within."

★ Mix everything together in the bowl with a wooden spoon or a wooden stick. Turn the spoon or stick in a circular clockwise direction and while doing this, imagine that you feel a circle of energy moving from the bowl outwards, growing larger and larger until the visualized energy envelops your entire home.

★ Then pour the mixture into the glass jar and firmly screw on the lid. Leave the bottle near your front door for seven days, beginning this part of the spell by saying:
"By the power of seven by seven, the spell has been cast, O blessed be."

SPELL DISPOSAL

By the eighth day, the spell has served its purpose, so wrap the bottle in newspaper and throw it away into the trash or, if you prefer, you may bury it in your backyard.

MAGICAL INGREDIENTS

★ 1 teaspoon dried onion powder

★ wooden bowl

★ 1 teaspoon ground rosemary

★ 1 teaspoon dried ginger (or a couple of slices of fresh ginger)

★ 1 teaspoon dill seeds

★ 1 teaspoon ground white pepper

★ 1 teaspoon aniseed

★ 1 teaspoon earth

★ wooden spoon or stick

★ clean glass jar with screw-top lid

Faerie Shake

This magical cocktail is pure and natural, and it has a dual purpose. Make it for an energy kick first thing in the morning, or as a relaxing night-time soother.

MAGICAL INGREDIENTS

★ 2½ cups cold milk

★ 1 teaspoon honey

★ 1 teaspoon vanilla essence

★ dash of nutmeg

★ 5 drops pink or lavender food coloring (preferably the natural vegetable variety)

★ My Scottish grandmother used to whip up this enchanted recipe for me when I was a child, especially when she felt I needed a bit of "laughing medicine." It has been in our family for generations, and is said to have been originally passed down to our Isle of Sky clan, from the Faerie Queen herself. It still manages to give me a delightful and magical boost before setting out for a busy day at work. Of course, children always love it, and in winter you can also enjoy it as a soothing and cosy nightcap by heating the milk slightly and serving it warm.

CAST THAT SPELL!

This delicious drink is good whenever you need a zing in your step, or a comforting bedtime drink.

MAKE THAT SHAKE

Mix all the ingredients in a blender or stir briskly with an egg whisk. Then pour into a glass or china decanter and serve chilled (serves three to four).

This shake is simply the easiest way I know to put a day-long spring in your step.

Mini Charms and Quick Tips

MAGIC HOME TIPS

A happy and healthy home means a happy and healthy you. So surround yourself with good energy and create a positive effect.

★ Paint your front door or window shutters any shade of blue. Or put something blue, like furniture, a plant pot, or sculpture near your front step.

★ Hang up some wind chimes near a window or doorway, somewhere where they can catch the flow of any breeze. This is a beautiful and simple way to help attract positive spirits and magical feelings into your home.

★ Fill your home with plenty of magical white candles of all shapes and sizes. Once a week, light a candle and for a few moments let your mind flow with positive thoughts.

★ Place two crossed wooden sticks (popsicle sticks are fine) in a shoe box near your front door—this will help keep negative vibes from entering your home.

★ To scatter any negative energies around your home and send them away, simply stand inside your house or apartment and slam your front door six times.

CIRCLES

Cleansing circles are made by sweeping brooms counterclockwise around any room of your home. Prosperity circles are made by swooshing a broom or some salt around your home in a clockwise direction.

Turn even a small kitchen, balcony, or courtyard into a mini witchy garden by stocking up with lots of little pots of your favorite home-grown herbs and fresh or dried flowers.

ENCHANTED WOODS

Here are some tips on the enchanted characters of different types of wood.

RATTAN, WICKER, OR CANE: an ancient magical material, to enhance spellcasting and good fortune in the home.

EBONY: represents high magic energy and protection.

OAK: this was Merlin's "Great Tree" of magic; brings strength and healing.

PINE: attracts money, purification, and healing.

REDWOOD: is said to lengthen the home dweller's life cycle.

CHERRY: known for centuries to fill the house with love and sexual passion.

TEAK: improves money-making and success.

CEDAR: this woody aroma and vibration brings peacefulness and protection.

MAHOGANY: the glow from this kind of wood encourages better health and tranquility.

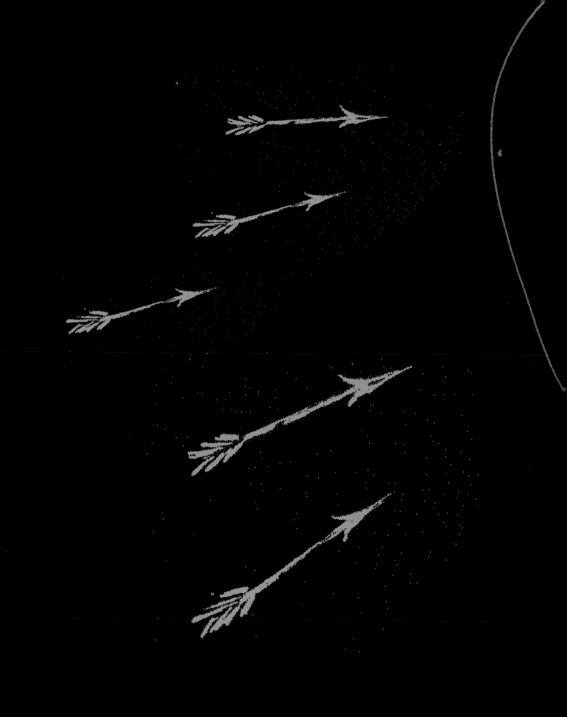

get even

But no-one gets HURT

Hex Away

CAUSE BAD
LUCK TO BOUNCE
STRAIGHT OFF

MAGICAL INGREDIENTS

★ fresh ginger root or 1 teaspoon bottled ginger

★ some seaweed, straight from the sea if possible but you can just as easily use seaweed from a nori roll or sushi paper (bought in health food stores or Asian food stores) or some that's canned or bottled

★ any kind of water (pond, lake, or even a filled bathtub!)

If your wish is to get rid of a jinx, or when you think someone is sending you shadowy bad vibes, then cast this spell to help you out of that tough spot.

★ At twelve o'clock on a Sunday afternoon, find a stretch of water. Don't worry if you don't live near a river, sea, or lake. Just use your imagination—even a filled bathtub sprinkled with a touch of salt will do.

★ Stand near the water (be careful to stay safe if you're outdoors) holding the ginger and either the nori paper or seaweed in your right hand. Breathe calmly and relax for a minute while focusing on peaceful and serene thoughts. As you gaze into the water, repeat this incantation:
"By the Gods of the Wind and Sea,
ill wind and conflict is banished,
and sent far away from me."

CAST THAT SPELL!

Best time to begin your anti-hex magic is midday on any Sunday of the month.

★ Throw the ginger and the nori paper into the water, then close your eyes and imagine that you are strolling along a beach, a warm breeze blowing through your hair. Imagine you are having a great time, feeling completely refreshed and untroubled and free of worries.

And when you're done, simply rinse off any residual bad luck with the deepest, fizziest bubble-bath you can confect.

★ Wind up the final power of the spell by saying with confidence and conviction in your voice:

"Now I see reflected only serenity and affection. And so it is, it is so, And so mote it be... !"

SCOUR THAT TUB

If you have used a bathtub or a sink for the spell, pull out the plug and let all the water drain out, then throw away any leftover ginger or seaweed.

Bad Hair Day

Her theme song is "You're So Vain." She's as shallow as an empty swimming pool. The only way to get her attention is to talk about her and only her. And as soon as she can fit her generous butt into those brand new, size 4 hipsters, she's gonna look exactly like Jennifer Lopez. Yeah right. Quick! Do the girl (and the rest of us) a big favor! For her sake and for the "good of all," it's time to brew up this "hey girl, what's up with your hair?" charm. It's harmless and lasts only for one day.

Anyone who's so completely caught up with their mirror image may find a well-deserved lesson in this great anti-grooming spell.

MAGICAL INGREDIENTS

★ doll (preferably one that has been used or bought from a second-hand store)

★ 1 teaspoon of salt

★ one or two dog hairs

★ tube of eyelash or nail glue

★ mirror

★ spring water

SHARE THE HAIR CARE HEX

★ Find a quiet space where you can perform your magic ritual and place all your ingredients onto a table or the floor. Begin your spell by sprinkling a circle of salt on the floor around you in a clockwise direction. Next, hold the doll in both hands and say:

"I cast this spell in the name of good, no harm will be done, O blessed Be."

★ Next, stick the dog hair onto the head of the doll with the glue and let it dry for a few moments. Then, take the doll and sit on the floor inside the circle of salt. Meditate for a few moments and then say these magical words.

"Just for today, just for
a day, when you look in
the mirror you will see
your true way.
Step back from your self
and look into the light,
the hair is a mess, but
your soul will be right."

★ Now place the doll in front of a mirror and leave it there all night and the following day. It's a one-day spell only so at midnight the following evening pull the dog hairs off from the doll's head and throw them away. Sprinkle the doll with a bit of salt to cleanse it. Then give its hair a quick wash in some spring water, towel dry, and voila-your doll is back to her beautiful (hopefully more real) self.

The best ever familiar is a cat with Sicilian connections.

Totally Toady

MAGICAL INGREDIENTS

★ piece of paper with his name written on it in black pen

★ 1 garlic clove peeled (or 1 teaspoon garlic paste)

★ 1 teaspoon spring or mineral water

★ 1 teaspoon cod liver oil

★ 1 teaspoon dried rosemary

★ yellow feather (any kind of feather will do)

★ screw-top jar

You know the type. You don't have to turn this one into a toad—because he already is one! He's that slimy guy at work who just won't keep his hands to himself. To add to the insult, he's real sneaky and nobody else seems to have noticed what's happening (although if he could read the walls of the women's bathroom, he'd learn a good thing or two). This spell will give you the inner strength to speak out and confront the issue—as an added magical bonus, it can also compel the cowardly cad to reveal his true toady nature to all and sundry.

If you need to make a quick potion in the office kitchen, be clean and tidy—LEAVE NO TRACES.

CAST THAT SPELL!

The best time to cast this spell is anytime on a weekday.

REVEAL HIS INNER TOAD

★ Place all of your ingredients into the jar and firmly twist on the lid. Then shake it for a moment while you say this incantation out aloud:

"With this elixir I now declare, that it shall repel the toad and reveal the lecher, With the best intentions and for my welfare. If you touch me again, retribution shall be here."

★ The next day, wrap the jar up in a plastic bag (or transfer some of the potion into your phial from this spell pack) and take it to work with you in your bag or briefcase. At some stage during the day, walk just once around your desk in a counterclockwise direction while carrying the bag (you can leave it inside your purse or briefcase if you like).

★ Finally, take the jar home with you that evening and bury it in the ground somewhere near the front of your home. Leave it buried until the spell has worked its purpose—afterwards you can dispose of the jar in a garbage can.

Revel in the knowledge that soon he must reveal his true nature to all.

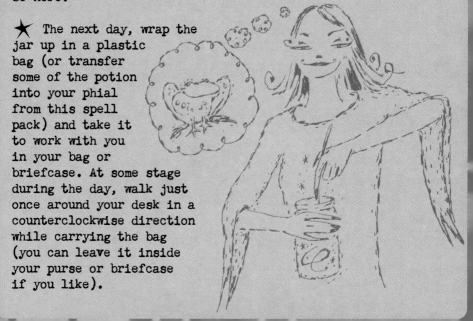

web Stalker

Eeeuuuwww, some creep's been following you around or leaving nasty messages. Well, apart from all the essential obvious things you can do, like making sure people close to you know about it, and using your good sense—witchy people should be just as logical as everyone else—this ritual helps give a magical backup to any practical anti-stalking steps you're gonna take.

Stay calm and tranquil. You can rid yourself of this virtual pest with just a little help from your feline friend.

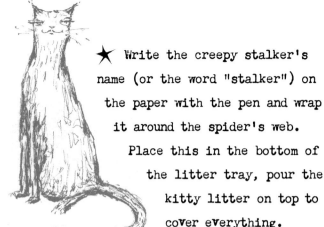

★ Write the creepy stalker's name (or the word "stalker") on the paper with the pen and wrap it around the spider's web. Place this in the bottom of the litter tray, pour the kitty litter on top to cover everything.

CAST THAT SPELL!

Weave this spell on a Saturday or the night of a full moon.

★ Next, let your, or a friend's, kitty use as per normal. When the tray is dirty enough (the cat will be sure to tell you when it is) then throw the dirty litter and paper in the garbage. The tray can be put back to every day use by just washing it out with warm soapy water. And please don't forget to thank good ol' kitty for a job well done!

MAGICAL INGREDIENTS

★ piece of a spider's web (a real one is great or you can also buy the party store variety that's used a lot at Halloween—it can be either canned, paper, or plastic)

★ piece of brown paper (from a grocery bag is fine)

★ black pen

★ some clean kitty litter

★ litter tray

THE SIDE EFFECTS

★ Only visible side effects are: (a) possible fits of laughter (you—not them) and

(b) occasional coughing up of fur balls (the stalker—not you).

★ 83 ★

Hush Up

ZIP THAT LIP

Backstabbing gossipers, sheesh!
What a pain in the neck they can be!
Especially when they pretend to be your
best friend, sucking up to you so they
can get to hear your inner most secret
thoughts and then, hey presto! They
take great delight in going around town
stirring up trouble and strife. Well,
here's a spell an old
wizard taught me that
is just the ticket for
hushing up loose lips
and those lying rat-
finks— don't stress,
it won't hurt anyone
(it just helps to
dissolve their
desire to hurt and
malign you—a noble
cause if ever
there was one!).

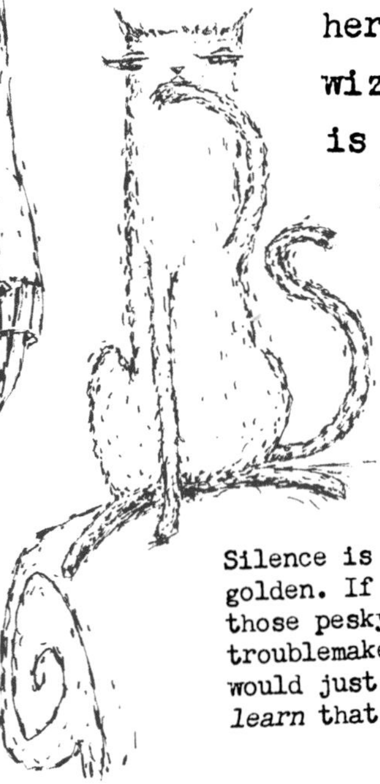

Silence is
golden. If
those pesky
troublemakers
would just
learn that.

★ Place the spell items into your cauldron (any old kitchen pot will do) and take the pot outside as the sun is setting and stand facing West. While you stir the magic formula, say:

"I mix to fix in the name of good.
Cease your lies [say the name of the person].
Each time you gossip and say more than you
    should, back to you threefold your
    mischief returns.
No harm will be done to me or to another
but a lesson will be learned, and deserve
    it you would."

★ Next, pour everything into a plastic bag and tie up the end and leave it all outside until nine in the evening. When it's after nine o'clock, the magic has gone out into the universe, so you can get rid of the bag. Just throw it away into the trash.

CAST THAT SPELL!

An hour before the sun sets, gather these items of magic.

MAGICAL INGREDIENTS

★ 1 cup of salt

★ $\frac{1}{2}$ cup of red wine (the cheaper the better)

★ nail clippings from the toe nails on your left foot (just the big toe will do)

★ and a leftover barbecued or fried chicken leg

★ 85 ★

Night Queen

Cast this spell and dance your way past the velvet ropes at all your favorite hangouts and clubs. And don't be surprised if that troublesome Maitre d', suddenly starts remembering you by your first name, and ushering you over to the best table in the house.

MAGICAL INGREDIENTS

★ pair of high-heeled or stiletto shoes (any color will do, but black or scarlet red would be just perfect)

★ your favorite red lipstick

★ black evening bag

★ fan (an inexpensive one or either a lacy Spanish-style or a simple paper Asian-style fan, both of which can be easily hired or purchased from party stores or costume shops)

★ glitter (optional)

★ When it's seven in the evening, take a shower or bath and after you have patted yourself dry, remain skyclad and get dressed in just your high-heel shoes. Then go stand in front of a mirror holding the red lipstick in your right hand as you charge it with magical energy with this incantation:

"O magic goddess, traveler of the mystic night, grant me charisma and surround me in light."

CAST THAT SPELL!

At seven o'clock, on the evening you plan to go out.

★ Next, look at your reflection in the mirror and make up your mouth with the lipstick. When you have finished applying the red lipstick, put it into the black evening bag. Next go and pick up the fan in your right hand, waving it up in the air and around your head and body in a clockwise circle as you repeat these words:

> "With a wave and a walk I shall travel
> through my chosen door.
> All ways shall be open and glamour's
> power will be in store."

★ Next, finish getting ready as normal, by applying your makeup and getting fully dressed in your best outfit. But don't forget to put the red lipstick in your bag, and be sure to carry the fan with you (either in your hand or inside the handbag) when you arrive at the club or restaurant. If you like, you may also sprinkle some glitter over your bag and shoes just before you leave for your night on the town.

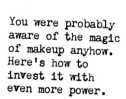

You were probably aware of the magic of makeup anyhow. Here's how to invest it with even more power.

Out of the Bag

UNMASK THE
JOKER IN
YOUR PACK

MAGICAL INGREDIENTS

★ any photographs of the people you suspect

★ wooden clothes pin

★ indoor or outdoor clothes line

★ black pepper shaker

Got the feeling there's a traitor in your midst? Something smells in the State of Denmark, but you just can't put your finger on who's the rotten egg? To help expose spies and disloyalty, cast this spell on the first or last Saturday of any month, and watch the proverbial cat crawl out of the bag.

CAST THAT SPELL!

Best time to cast the spell is on the first or last Saturday of any month.

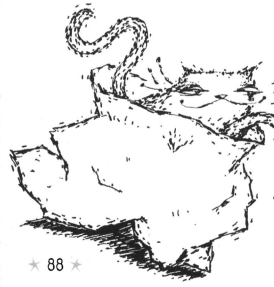

★ Outdoors is best for this, but if you can't go outside, make sure you hang the clothes line near a window for moon energy.

The truth may hurt—but if there's disloyalty around it really *is* better to know.

Take the photographs and pin them onto the clothes line with the wooden pin. Then stand close by and sprinkle the pepper around yourself in a counter-clockwise circle as you say these words aloud:

"Lies BE GONE cheater BE revealed,
deception is uncovered and now your
    fate is sealed,
come into the light, come into the light,
    it will be made right,
THE SPELL IS NOW DONE, SO IT SHALL BE REAL!"

★ Next, leave the photographs overnight to be charged by lunar energies (you can wrap the photos in a plastic bag or plastic wrap if you are concerned about rain) and clean up any leftover pepper.

★ The next day, unpin the pictures, throw away the clothes pin and place the photos inside a brown paper bag. Then place the bag in a safe place where it will not be disturbed and leave it there for as long as it takes (the spell's energy will last up to three months).

SPELL DISPOSAL

Anytime after the spell has performed its magical duties, you may unwrap the photos, throw away the paper bag and sprinkle any wanted photos in salt to cleanse and purify. Then you can put them safely back in their usual place.

Mini Charms and Quick Tips

THE RIGHT FRIGHT NIGHTS

Here are some great times for weaving anti-stress spells. To get the most out of your spell casting, pick the right time to get witchy...

SATURDAY

★ Luckily for us enchanted ones, this power day of the planet Saturn comes around every week. Its strong planetary influence is great for weaving away worries, and exposing witch hunters.

HALLOWEEN

★ This is an absolutely perfect time (especially at midnight) for casting both protection and banishing spells.

YOU ARE READY FOR CLOSURE WHEN...
You no longer actually spit when you talk about him

You laugh at the thought of what his next girlfriend's in for.

DARK OF THE MOON

★ This one's for experienced hexers only. Use only in emergencies (like staving off stalkers and other weirdos).

SUNSET

Wickedly inspirational time for banishing unwanted energies, bringing resolution and closure on painful issues and past mistakes (both yours and theirs).

THREE O'CLOCK IN THE MORNING

Powerful energies abound at this often overlooked witching hour. Like midnight, it is a superb time for binding spells and naughty notions.

CANNY COMPONENTS

These are some ancient ingredients plus a few modern-day bits and pieces for brewing up all kinds of helpful but harmless, hex therapy.

* garlic
* cayenne pepper
* black pepper
* ginger
* high-heeled black shoes
* dog or cat hair
* handful of earth
* leftover chicken bones (wash them thoroughly if you're keeping in storage)
* sweaty t-shirt
* dirty gym socks
* broomstick

* cauldron
* mortar and pestle
* glass or metal jars, and your magic potion phials
* embarrassing photographs (of those you wish to cast a spell on of course, not you!)
* the purple charm bag from your spell pack

Glossary

ALMANAC A year book of magical moon times, seasons, and festivals.

ALTAR A sacred space or table where spells can be cast and magical symbols and tools are stored and honored.

ARTEMIS Greek goddess of the moon.

DARK MOON Brief time where the moon does not reflect the sun and appears to only show its dark face to the earth.

DRUIDISM Based on the philosophy of Druid priests and priestesses, who were the advisors, magicians, teachers, and spiritual leaders of the pre-christian Celtic people of Ireland, Scotland, Gaul, Wales, and Southern Germany.

ESSENTIAL OILS The pure distilled oils and essences of plants, flowers,

bark, and herbs; commonly used in both aromatherapy and spellcasting.

FAMILIAR Any favorite animal with witchy or psychic abilities and symbolism, such as a cat, toad, snake, horse, or raven.

FOLK HEALING The oldest form of medicine and healing, which combines knowledge of herbalism with the powers of the mind, spirit, and mystical forces of nature.

FORTUNATA Ancient Roman goddess who rules good luck and fortune.

FULL MOON Magical time when the moon reaches its full face, the height of light reflection, and earthly influence.

HALLOWEEN This celebration falls on October 31st and is based on the ancient Celtic festival of Samhain,

(a time when both the spirit and earthly realms are close together).

HEX The transferral of bad luck onto another person.

ISIS Ancient Egyptian goddess of magic and feminine power.

JINX A curse or constant bad luck.

MERCURY The planet of communication and travel and the Roman god of thought and speed.

MERLIN The personification of the ultimate wizard, teacher, and fatherly guide to the ways of Old Sorcery.

NEW MOON The rebirth phase of the moon's cycle as it grows back towards full moon power.

QUARTZ CRYSTAL Magical stone of intense earthly light and natural energy. Used often to empower

magic wands and spellcasting.

SKYCLAD Originally a mystical Indian term that was later translated into modern witchcraft to mean "naked" or "dressed in nothing but the sky and stars."

VENUS Roman equivalent to Goddess Aphrodite, the powerful diva of love, beauty, and sexuality.

WANING MOON Shrinking phase after the full moon.

WAXING MOON Growing phase after the dark and new moon.

WICCA Ancient Sanskrit word meaning "wise one." Later adapted into old English meaning "to weave" and "witch."

ZODIAC Band in the heavens divided into 12 signs. These birth signs reflect various human traits and influence lives.

Further Information

For updates and information
on witchy ways, magical
message boards, and Deborah's
Magic Music CD, visit her
website www.deborahgray.com

To have a spell especially
designed for you, send
your inquiries to
spell@deborahgray.com

OTHER BOOKS BY DEBORAH GRAY

How to Turn Your Ex-Boyfriend
into a Toad *(HarperCollins,
New York, 1996)*

Nice Girl's Book of Naughty
Spells *(Charles Tuttle Co.,
Boston, 1999)*

How to Turn Your Boyfriend
into a Love Slave
(HarperCollins, New York, 2000)

Good Witch's Guide to
Wicked Ways *(Charles Tuttle
Co., Boston, 2001)*

How to Be a Real Witch
(HarperCollins, Sydney, 2001)

To find these and other
magical books on-line visit
www.barnes&noble.com

If you're looking for
hard-to-find witchy herbs
and spell ingredients, go
to www.whitemagic.com.au

Index

THE AUTHOR

"Good Witch," Deborah Gray was initiated as a teenager into a Magical Druid Circle in the 1970s and has inherited her knowledge of metaphysics and magic through the rare and respected apprenticeship method while dedicating years of study alongside one of the world's few remaining Druid Masters. She is an award winning songwriter and metaphysical lecturer and is the author of four internationally best selling books, (*Nice Girl's Book of Naughty Spells, How to Turn Your Ex-Boyfriend Into a Toad, Good Witch's Guide to Wicked Ways, How to Turn Your Boyfriend Into a Love Slave*). Her magical words have been translated into nine different languages and continually excite and inspire the imaginations of her readers throughout the U.S., United Kingdom, France, Germany, Spain, Japan, Australia, and many other countries around the world.

ACKNOWLEDGEMENTS

This book is dedicated to you dear reader-may you always enjoy the magic you find within its pages, and be inspired by the knowledge that each and every spell has been magically crafted in the name of good and to harm none. O blessed be.